Piezo

Piezo
©2014 by Russell Buker

Published by the Piscataqua Press
An imprint of RiverRun Bookstore, Inc
142 Fleet St. | Portsmouth, NH | 03801

www.piscataquapress.com
www.riverrunbookstore.com

"The Apple Tree" and "Tete Dure," were previously printed in the *Off the Coast Review*

Printed in The United States of America

PISCATAQUA
PRESS

Piezo

Poems by

Russell Buker

To DeWitt Hardy

Teacher/mentor in my journey

Forward:

    Silence took my tongue in the ending of my other life. Outside never moved but I squirmed a lot, never, no, never, wondering why is it that most poets fear, an uneasiness, that one day we will be revealed to have been totally unconcerned in a foolish or unnecessary adventure.

    I who riot just to the left of leprechauns in ecstasy have watched the forests of my state fill by degrees with decreed writers should be angered but am amazed at the amount of leaves left over for visitors seeking the honest silence of yesterday's library's cozy air that induces a welcomed drowsiness allowing words to well up through the blank pages' fabric in my puzzled face.

    The third form of dread is doubt or despair and I was told to use less emotion and more feeling as feeling is of a more sophisticated cognition. Finally, I rest as I now realize that my fear has been overcome by procedure, as soldiers are taught also, where any of my poetical emergencies were dwarfed by simple rewriting or starting another poem fearing the outcome or, yes, my outcome as I write through the fogs of dread in silence.

    I had just delivered a commencement speech at a high school that I had taught in for a considerable time and one of the teachers asked what I was doing in my retirement. Oh, I have been writing and writing books of poetry, I replied. Why on earth would you do that, he asked, nobody reads poetry anymore. The academic system grinds out way too many poets/writers every year and they in turn grind out obligatory work to be printed in the industry of presses that has been created to accommodate them. Passionless stuff, passion matters in poetry and one of the many reasons poetry seemingly inspires so little passion among people in contemporary society is that it has ceased communicating with people and is much too concerned with just acceptance in its industry.

I think I forgot this arguing back and forth. Reality is flexible and depends where you are. I'm not attempting to sell and realize my audience so far is small, but I enjoy writing, nor do I worry about my window of opportunity as I find the value of credit is actually in the doing. I also agree with Yeats' sentiment as he looked around his club in Dublin where the poets hung out" there are too many of us" but with my being away from the mainstream, for the most part, I would hesitate to be the one who says, You stay, You go. No thank you I'm off to feed my feral cats. They are the real poets.

—Russell Buker

Table of Contents

1 | You Were

Waving in this
breeze
snow crusted
with-
out cloth. Held
by
snow the broken
branch
appears to be
stuck
in our shed
roof
on a flagship day.

Your
brother said to
us:
Useful uselessness.

I
sat all last night
again
listened to slow
voices
streaming from the North-
East
and googled your site
to see
if you were outside
shoveling
but all the pointer
shows
is fuzzy foreground
before
you bought the place
with
our own money

2 | Suddenly

Water
suddenly coming,
it
could only happen
in
a poem by a friend who
who
Serves un-cracked, brain-
wall-
nuts, laughs to see my
swallow
by tilting puffed head
back
and forth while gulping,
enabling
glottal freedoms and
wheezing
how good this tastes
while
our dumb ancestral
brute's
fingers dipping bubbly
cracked
cranium blood and turning
to
a mate knowing she will
now
receive more from him

3 | Clear

This game is now ex-
travagant:
there are not many
300
hitters at home

All I can do is
pray
for another cure,
word,
that follows from

first to third with an
eye
still on the ball
other
on the excited third

base coach plus a
foot
pounding in my ears
with
breath held for a clear
signal

4 | Armed-Aurora

How I would like
to buzz
with the unseen oak
leaf
tonight, armed only
with
a planetarium light
for
night talking in the
favored
solar message. In this outside
room

of hanging, slow greens a
dementia
hangs within the eyes of
all
beholders rustling slowly
in
spite of our knowing
how
protected we were,
are,
and hopefully will
be

5 | Room

With
the first step:
still
sleeping floor-
board
gives a welcome
bark,
self reflecting
after
all those previous
years

of
welcoming weight
as
a sign that every
frame
in both our life's
small
hotel has seemed
orderly
even before I went
away

6 | Superb

Call this my break
during
Februa as I now eat
smart
bagels at nine AM

Ah
that golden crust that
boiled,
baked both face's good
bye

recognizes how bloody
we
can be with a mere
Lux
of our changing voices

Gentle Gentile, simalcas and
janitor
obsessed with the noise
almost
clean makes. All the cities

I've
readily lived in are merely
different
birds huddled in their
dark

waiting sun and flight
and
the lonely janitor again
sweep-
mopping-mopping up

the
debris, sweet guano,
of
the bird-beak's incessant
pecking

during sunlit hours
while
becoming way too fat
for
night- grey flights

7 | Winter Silences

My favorite winter
silence
stares back at
me
from inside my
large
maple tree, under
ice
covering the lake.

It
seems so immobile
now
that I fear ever
getting
them back or patiently
praying
for their return
while

above in the convex
sky,
Mughal, is cloudy
also
not bothering to
reflect
either one of me
and
songs seems frozen

8 | Cure

Time grows monstrous
slow over igneous,
high altitude beds

The gneiss pathway
through crystal, green
algae of mountain wintering

has turned pinkish,
watermelon snow,
as a sun block

melting the snow and
blooming an uncanny
taste of the real thing

Feeding ice worms,
snow fleas with laxative
effect for the ravenous

oxygen deprived
Komen bypassers
looking for their cure

without the beaurecratic
empires sanctimonious collections,
tions with friendly salaries

9 | Experience

Also
learned early on to
see
through the spaces
allowed
between ice crystals
on
the car wind-shield

I was so young
Then;
just had fallen out
of
a clump of young
maples
that my neighborhood
friends

were challenge climbing
and
laid there looking
up
at the comforting
sky
even though my right
arm

now hurting worse than
I
could have imagined.
What
struck me was that my
soul,
flowing through bone-
marrow,

remained even, even in
this
odd shaped arm,
sign
surely that attendant, blue
skies
were not about to give
up

on finding me
no
matter how much I
break
or the resetting
goes

10 | Clinging

Sleep was out of the
question,
hospitals are never
quiet,
the noise I heard
on
every street, road,
comes
back in thin, colored
drips
of glowing tungsten,
aspirin
really, as I flew
by
graves--a wild finger
sliding
through clinging dust
on
grandmother's antique chair—

Graves
puddled along thoroughfares,
night
lights shining with collected
Sun,
gifted to leaden snow determined
to hold
on. No matter how well
I
held on, how many hospitals
lived
in, the wounds always came
back
as I waited all day, all day.
My chance
death on the operating table
only
to be sent back to my waiting
ward

11 | The Apple Tree

Unaware the old apple tree
dropped a few scraggly fruit
at its feet and no one had
bothered to pick them up

Unaware that at this time
last year the old barn
had fallen before the
weight of winter snows

Unaware that this season
marked twenty-five years
since the last farm tenant
had moved closer to town

Unaware that some one
was taking a picture
where it had once stood
its ground as long as possible

12 | Perception

Gateway to the unseen bottom
falling out, hurt fabric,
triple moon reflected occupying
the room of the big windows
and my antic oscillations

I who had to relearn nightly
to cast unarmed, imaged perfection,
feeling next to nothing in my
my right arm, alertly watch
as the realistic fly I hurl

looks for a soft landing
with eyes on me as if
applause is its real goal
or the cast has gone awry,
thankfully not in the alders

again, with hope of catching
the fish out of its pasture

13 | Cornea

My cornea's so clouded
that sun spots claimed
to be double barreled
aiming at all of me

strikes brazen laughing
as one barrel seems
so square that its
pattern will probably miss

by quite a bit yet if I
unwillingly flinch the
other is sure to be very
right on bulls eye target

the same way the heart
shaped coronal mass
ejection was on February
the 14th and I die again

14 | Money Spent

Money spent on the stars
is a good thing. Yes.

I sit in my bright hotel
room looking out

the window at a brick
wall of linear, colored

red stars and wonder if
anyone in the audience

tonight was thinking the same
as light pollution had obliterated

all the stars in the planetarium
while I recited my poems

For god's sake turn the stars
back on my mind yelled

for that is where these poems came
from and will return in the whisper

of a solar flare glancing off
a magnetic field as quickly

as the tip money left at my dinner
goes into a special waitress pocket

15 | Left Hand For Les

My cat and I are so
like Oscar Wilde,
in a difficult way,

the cat's so lazy
he lies on the porch
waits for a bird to

stun itself by flying
into the big windows
then calmly walks over

picks it up, takes it
to the wildlife crossing
tells it all about

little Red Riding Hood
and the wolfing wolf
crying" Gad that was awful! "

To say nothing about how
I wish I'd said that
before it was too late

I too sit on the same
sun porch reading volumes
swallowing various words

feathers and all until the cat
comes back with a retort
that I have it all wrong.

For you see the grandmother
and wolf were copulating until
she gasped and disappeared

How grim, how grim, I'll say,
how about the little girl? Oh
I've taken good care of him

16 | Incomprehensible

I worry about my lips
all the guilt, gonadual
squeeze, while dragging
beaver carcass out onto the
ice--clapping and oohing
with each eagle's soar and bite

All the guilt I've heard
about seem to be sliding
down my empty wine glass
gearing up to walk across
the sandy beach into
seemingly receptive sea

There is enough sin on
and in this slippery sea
to make one fear falling
asleep even knowing its
absence leads to early
onset aspirational dementia

Oh yes, I worry about my
lips, wordless at times,
and how you have to fill
in crunchy, sand words
for me when I'm telling
you how it is, was whet

17 | Catching up

I was a long time
gambler,
vaultless, who was
unafraid
to jump from any cliff
to another
with one eye shut and
tuning
out all the don'ts
from
bellowing below.
Whose
other eye steered
arm
and pen into the open
page
where I could never
catch
up with one don't

18 | Indecisions

When I returned
to the sunny deck,
interrupted by robo-
call, I saw two red
squirrels fighting
over my coffee

Shabos goy was all
I could think of
while they staggered,
highly caffeinated, off
unable to climb a tree
for their safekeeping

A wise man would
have helped them.
I poured my coffee
on the melting snow.
Shabos and goy would
your mom be proud.

19 | Silene Stenophylla

Oh no, not again
not another Carnival

We're staying locked
in this ice as long as

it lasts. No more cookies
and milk sweetened dreams

No more birds, mastodons,
flowers flying out

of the cozy ice. No
more die-offs for us

or more cycles of re-
generation and death

Leave us alone. You
are on your own ice-

less brink and we do
not want to watch

Cover us with your lab
coat and try to walk

back in the rapidly
warming permafrost

20 | Birch

All that remains is
wall of wind and light

before last year's
long, arid dry and

in the buy and sell
of late winter storms

bare ground was
at a premium here

The mostly white trees
sang again in

breathable phrases
onto the stark

birch starch with
black branch bowls

collecting weak heat
for bell weather roots

motioning each other
to move the lace race,

rootlets frenzy, before
hypotaxic-sun and

the grass that hugs
the trunk shamelessly

withers the tree and
nesting's of birds

Elegant firewood
for shivering fireplace

21 | Totem Talk

Heaped high on everyone
in a lost lineage and
even though I tried
to time my breath
with every gust,
every gentle breeze

and glared back at
the sun with smooth,
forehead messages.
The constant rains
of all my yesterdays
broke slowly through

my smile, planting
furroughs on my face
to an unrecognizable
blur, an oddity, in the same
way that The Old Man
Of Cannon Mountain

came to know a different
life in the silence of
jumbled scree. I too miss
reverential stares,
wonder who will come forth
carve the new totem

22 | Romance

Nestled in
romantic out-
skirts beyond
the beyond of sun-
blurbs quiet
hum waiting
for the Ravens
to come in
off the ice
I sit on old
Norse Thrones
that drunkenly
washed ashore

so far from home.
not one to bemoan
spilt beverage
near its intended
caress I watch
and wait my dim
turn to talk
my bright friend's
ear off about
another night
missed out on
staying out of
the way

23 | ..)

I am all ears, both,
and saliva. Who would
not be searching this
certain un-knowable,
such a change, a soft
footstep behind. I am
out of kilter. Finally
clouds shifted--this
February conjunction
was supposed to shine
through clouds and light
pollution the way pain
squirts from hurt and
I climb the little knoll
beside the dark lawn
search the many reasons
that now open one by one
and western bearing Venus,
Jupiter and morsel of moon
form their uncomplicated
triangle sight angles

24 | They came

They came to this country
on a song, doin and hopin.
All that I'm hopin, predicting
dreams relevance to be more
alive coming from the remaining
front steps in a changing landscape
powerless in the power of whales
that skipped out of our school
long ago for enormities sake

They came to this country,
still bug-eyed from their not
me, can't be land of leveled fields,
with clumps of resume reference
stuck on elegant dance- boots,
romantic stories stalking through
wet-shine of this or that year's
choice of godly grain turn
inward in the awed silence every

morning sorting the pills for blood
pressure, sugar coating the routine
that sugar needs to play in this
reminisce of a youthful bliss
etched somewhere in perseverance
of fairly out, fairly in, looking
forward today, paralytic, with
a solitary cup of earnest human
hopin everything galls down

25 | So Many

Days comes quicker
so many aunts away
at this time of year
this is it for us, pegs
in the rafters holding on

but the weather's gone
wild into an uncertain
spring again allowing
grey wolves to seem white
in the morning gloom

lips curled back in their
own hunger exposing red
moon's glow in long teeth
Food in the cellar's scant
and changing into its own,

own death song, while
food on the hoof shrinks
inedible into its own blood and
kitchen window's no longer
friendly quietly watching the

wolves gathering in binding
 hedgerows that limit field's
spreading out and luxuriating
in the breaks of prescriptive light,
sun warm southern air

26 | Say

Say goodbye to the plucking.
I am way too weak have
to stumble down off the roost

as that appeared to be the easiest
approach to you and yet my
joy of being here, unrehearsed,

among all my plans--definitely
not quite the same person
I was supposed to be--spooky

place with sun reflecting
redirecting my stories of
outside and thumb cracks

Every winter with brinicle
ice stalactite's deadly creep
over skins toughest flesh,

made worse by the inedibility
of fresh eggs and a methodical,
slow, fox-tight- hatchet groan

27 | Who said

Why wouldn't, shouldn't
we know,
whether we can read
or not.
Our exclusion zones will
somehow
overlap, as an ounce
put in
a glass too soon becomes
a quart
of sliced words out
of
sun- conversationals,
plasma,
fetal waves, tear
across
space between us
and full,
whitened moon, unheard,
unseen,
still gaining speed
glancing
off and amusing space
darkness
without as much as a
whoa
did you all hear that,
see that

28 | Wonder

I wonder if he
was listening to
the notes played
by the fingers he
was ordered to
cut off or if perhaps
the whole piece

I wonder if he
was listening to
his commandant's
voice, You Vill, Ya,
telling him to cut
certain fingers off
this Jew Bastard

who refused to play
justifiable propaganda
and then when fingers,
between thumb and middle,
fell to the ground disappearing
in the crowd and who brought
bare bones into the chamber

Not the whole
story of your
wasted waiting
between the ordinary
and ecstatic rain's
attempt to soften
autistic arias of birds
outlined in pond
ice, immobile for
the moment, as they
wait without flutter
or mother to please:
she is immobilized
herself in love ground
fine with daily making
less from less and less
waiting for her man

30 | They

They came to me all
at once,
strange web, talking
of tensile
strength and how I
should
remain, relaxed and
unconscious--
this is my thoughts
willing
suspension, woof,
that
I rely upon, stone-held
brook--
until their donation
of time,
arbitrary, became less
impatient
than words could bear
and I
unravel just in time
to bring
accented air that I
love to
breathe from under
that
web one by one

31 | They Said

My latest hospital trip
was to test
a new machine that had
been invented
after my last operation.
They said
make your brain quiet--
a not unwelcome emptiness--
and yet
it never is, therefore
the horror
of what I can not
see is
observed at a safe
distance
by my doctors and MRI
Technicians
who watch expectantly as a
poem appears
on their imaging screen
without
so much as a rise in my
blood-pressure.

Indigo
shadows print out
the words
and silence falls slowly
throughout,
within except the gentle
whir
of a motor's cooling fan
nd a
technician's caught breath.

32 | Large

Large birds always seem
so
vulnerable on the ground

In this jingle of a sleepless
city
as if monogamy was not

outdated
It is as though I am
being

charged for every caught
breath
I take by someone in my

dream:
of three strange men's
Susanna's

over me while a dark
bird
rises from the frozen

lake
of sleep to the bright ceiling
in loins

quiet winging rhythms
back
and forth again careful

not
to dampen any seething
black

feathers' online flower.
You,
words clicking, we were

supposed
to be border crossings for
each other

33 | Hey

Hey! There is a pencil
stuck in my painting of you
rabbit's tensile strength is gone
no more undulations

except waves at the edges.
Nurse, the woman in this
picture, looks at her dog
who looks to nuzzle her

bare leg as I did last night.
Who would do that to my
story? Who would do that
to my super solemn nurse

who now knows me
better than I do myself

34 | Always

In the reflective mist of becoming
something else always, always
something unbearable

to all but me empathizing
fescue in blueberry fields,
whale in clear waters

who dared to walk themselves
from starry milky-way, cashing
in the promise of size, flying,

cleaner sidewalks and futures
anonymity, talking through
zonal changes in the water

that the worst times are over
or have they have just begun

35 | Bread

I miss
the tree that was at my
window
and the staring contests with
big red
the stock-still squirrel

Now
I am able to shake
hands
with the red rash of my
mornings
unable to feel the waving

winds
and rains nor place those
crusts
of expected amazement
felt
watching Red's bobbing

cheeks
and cold eyes on me
as if
I was more or less his
reluctant
savior, mostly less

now
that the tree has been
taken
down by wind and rain
and I
had to cut it up for removal

A bird whose wings
had
frozen during winter
now
does not recognize
my selves,
have become song
between
unreflective silent stones
and water
an unknown current
that flows
past fortunate known's
in on
and on's quick tumble
to there

37 | These

These late nights,
angel breathing
on my shoulder,
we both can not
sleep stare onto
sliding darkness.

And I wonder if
the thoughts that
wander are coming
through you first
they sound so deep
traveling on gaze

in the atmosphere
between, where all
sense comes, our
sleeping bodies'
echoes as make up
all over my page

38 | Flash

It is the middle of the day
I
still shine my flashlight
because
though they will deceive me
those
eyes are still good when,

when there is that certain
some-
thing tail gaiting my
poems,
there and yet not there,
hiding
and seeking on a lonely

journey-
we were alone in
our
must be eventuality-
yet
I am still furiously
building

forts of words to hide
behind
also, constantly criss-crossing
the lake
leaving my scent trail
on
the smiling side of other

where
whistle walking's relatively
cane-
less and where flashlights
seem
so out of place before returning,
must

39 | Fish

I was young and terrified
of fishing by myself

the mists were supposed
to be a help sneaking up

on tail wagging brookies
instead I imagined a girl

flowing back and forth in
those mists who would

not look at me in her
search of the river

Twig I thought as something
tugged at my line and I

reeled in desperately-
what if it was her hunger

I had snagged on to?-
but no it was a double,

a line wrapped twig
with an eight inch brookie.

How I remember running
from that overgrown pasture

with the still hooked fish
knowing I was well watched

40 | Dialogue

Circumstance has gone
feral
in the midst of an
anecdote

two eagles contemplate
empty
nest as though it were
wild

or stick-like toy
given
to her by another,
long

gone, tempting her
compulsive
sway in this high strung
world

A falling amorous flight and
he
asks, what if they do come
back

41 | April Snow

When winter comes back
I can find company in
a blank web of unknowing

as unhurried, drifting
preservation of myself
publishes the words

where I am found again,
random, melting with
these final flakes falling

We had left the movie
hall
hours ago and I was
trying
to fall asleep again.
Where
were all my usual
slender
ladies who should over-
see
my sleeping, death-certainty
until
they, too tired to keep their
appointed
shifts, drew their starry
robes
up and over staring eyes
that
had watched and watched
so long
my breathless sleeping,

turning
now into a parade of
ex-
lovers standing motionless
pointing
ring-less fingers at me and
thought
I head one crying, sobbing
to
the others that this was
not
the Hollywood we had planned
on

It is cold and we close our
curtains
to conserve the house heat
and
earth-like we shiver and won't
watch
the long silence of dust-
making
rent by the pounding rain.
When
as if to assuage us
pools
of water flow with anti-
septic
gauze for awhile and then
pools
merge, kissing and hugging,
one
another with youthful arms
before
the real movement started
and water
began to flow in earnest
seeking
to hide accumulating hides
that
were once our own bodies
playing
Solitaire in the evening dust

44 | Tete Dure

It's all the marbles
of our youth again.

So opposable
everything contested

or thought so little
of as to be not

worthy of bother.
Such is the pure joy

in our round circle's
mortal rollick

where agate rules
for eternity

45 | Wind

Wind direction is
always
from whence the
cat,
again, returned from

full flesh neon:
relative
images return.
They're
back, 50 %

off of sale price
so
whenever stranded
her
hand whistled into

a pocket book
took
confetti handfuls
watching
them slowly float

floor-ward, sidewalk,
where-
ever, whatever. You
bitch
a clerk yelled at

her silent smile
Red
covers my anger,
blue
my frustrations

while the rest
covers
most unfriendly
fears.
Broom, I'm not

crazy at all
just
need a broom
sorry
about that

46 | Super

Never sure if we
hear
the wind or some-
one
driving down our
lane

There is a fire
following
this strangeness
not
burning hot trees
but

cold as it tags
behind
our silent hearing
to
reflect in our eyes.
Company?

47 | Plus ca Change

To the lady that claims
to
not having a name

I can only marvel
at
how lonely, how sterile

she chooses her life
to be:
coming when called wife

or joy, with grief's slight
but
never NOW or bones flight,

futures heaven, sleepless night,

Stolen from the shores
rack
no thought of putting
back

such a wet stone, alone
where
nothing can, should atone

drying in the light of
night
smiling in the light of
night

Helen,
I never really
learned
my Latin and you
never
learned why.

Potted,
re-potted so many
times
new roots grew
through
the mass of strangled

ones
to collect all the
water
and stories needed in
turgid
race, eventual bloom.

Thankfully
the constrictions of
dead
roots stayed with
me
preventing desiccating

failures
from pot to pot-
your
translated test words,
phrases
we had not bothered
studying

49 | Inscape(GMH)

Oh well
that that monkish priest
could braze
his own nightmare into
our laps

Shanghaied,
you grumble awake:
awake
on a boat already far out
to sea

Landlubbered,
circumferential horizons
and swells
nearer his inattentive glad
you be

50 | Comme Ca

Wary as ever
and
not an ordinary
priest
yet possibly ordained
I have
fed bread to those
dark
shadowy birds
that
fly through and
behind
branches that remain
between
us in a game battle
of wits.
Lost before every
crust,
inclined to do
so,
rolled away from my
feet
according to the lay
of land

51 | Welcome

Welcome to our
humble-
the Raven's mock
fright
had circled a tight
circle,

came back to my
call
and I laughed for us
all--
the way we did
putting

stones in our snow-
balls
so very long ago
when
we were able to
throw

52 | They Sold Trigger

That movie hall's, where
we
used to gather from
surrounding
towns, been torn down
well
over ten years now

We rode with them
all:
Trigger and Buttermilk,
Champion,
Silver and Scout, Topper
always
with our white hats

so we could return
home
thrilled and content unaware
offshore
boardrooms were planning
leaving
those horses behind

vacationing in camo helmets,
exotic
places we did not belong

53 | Mend

I thought I'd
learn
how to do it

mended wings
ache
their aged way

through stormy
winds
that shafted

me to window's
reflection
She would appear

wonderful old
woman-
was it she

I always sought-
crates
me in such a tight

scold until all my
broken
bones had mended

then she would
teach
me to flail

all over again
mended
all over again

54 Haiku

riled air
over rankled water
poem spring

green leaves
I find our voice
in trees waters

to see the sea
whales are great friends
I know you know

feel me feel the sea
long-armed sand grains
desert swallowed

In the changing
air we saw sun's heat
reflect its sound

You never return
it's a gift you bring
all of us

When you go
who will replace water
in my tears

Silence in dark branches
are we any better off now
feeding these birds

dark night clouds
quietly break open
night's silence

55 | I Wandered

Into this jungle.
There
are large vowel
trees,
thinner consonant
ones
I
swear some leaves
resemble
punctuation marks

There is no sun-
light
down here nor
any
thing to eat
except,
possibly, myself
as
prey for there is
a

Burmese python
singing
to himself while
he
exercises vigorously
on
soggy leaf mold. He
knows
where I am, keeping
his

unblinking eyes on
me
daring me to move,
chew
leaves or follow
a
thin scraggily consonant
with
a hollow, frightened
vowel

56 | Murk

I had figured on isolation
saving me from elm bark
beetles

yet just across the lawn
or down the lane mail
awaits

Timothy Blackpool looking
out window pane, face's
held

between my shaking
hands, eyes always
surprised

how quiet the silence
in dark cedar branches
was

Are we any better off
now feeding these birds
from

the dark, where everything
comes, swells into its
own

space for as long as its
fluid is necessary before
gravitating

back to somewhere else,
another life to sustain
indifferent

page in indifferent books
I realize, once again,
tight

lipped smile, how much
a glass wearing copy
cat

I am, who probably
has spent way too much
on

new cabinets or a gun to
eradicate chipmunks from
my

floral gardens in the slow
gathering murky-shooting
mirkning

57 | Admit Impediments

Leave it be. Leave
contention
nor do I have any
desire
for a single reprieve.
Incessant
duty that I can
still
see, glass-less, movement
well
enough , venue to
venue,
without any blinking,
hemming,
hawing or asking
why
on earth have you
squandered
us so damn deliberately
with
your streak randomness
while
I mowed our lawn,
pyrrhic
solitude in the whirling
blades,
waiting, waiting, waiting

58 | How

Not many more sleepless
nights,
you'd think I'm disturbing
someone
else's dark deepwater
fishing.
Extemeophiles bob up,
float
by and I see vestige fish-
hooks,
spears-words already used-
in
determined blood-less
congealed
bodies with round, opaque
eyes
shunning the decency of a
blink.
They swim slowly through
my
vision before idling off
into
jelled nightscape under
piled
pillows and comforters

Closing the funeral home's
door
an unexpected noise
between
the doors slam and foot
steps

Neither of us remembered
why
but unable to earn onto the
music
all I could do was dance,
billowing

the music to clouds passing
into
sunshine on their way to
mountains
that make crying inevitable,
evitable

60 | Rae

Rae
Armantrout
knows
what this
is
all about

this thing
she
knows yet
wont
have to say

will
be with you
forever
and a day

remember our
wild
little river
damned

61 | By Now

Feather or
fuel
we would
take
the quicker
route

Clever dinosaurs
flew
into extinction
sixty
million years
before

we left the
coffee
shops in our
youth
and sat on a
La

Brea rim coolly
wanting
to go on a
record
never noticing
we

were settling
in
getting closer,
much
closer to sulfur's
songs

62 | Enemy

And its luminescent
snap
tattooing our trees, lungs

A sharp knife was used
to sever
his head from the body

Protest flags folded,
many
are now eager to claim

such a strong warrior's
jihad
over a completely unarmed

ransom less doctor who had
audacity
to return home from work

And the supposed enemy,
pockets
full, stare at their feet

hoping this incident will have
no
bearing on their cash flow

63 | Slight

Racing hallway's
light
I do not remember
anything
leaving this room

A hand, blue shoe's
maybe
Maybe kissing older
ladies,
gurney-ridden,

Goodbye,
goodbye

64 | Outside

Outside in the longer sun
with the addled bird- sky

the trees took the liberty
to use your electricity

and read your poetry
to myth myself again

argent assembled in
wrapped silken hugs

arriere-pensee
can not wait to hear

65 | Marginalia

Most children know
how
to fly, racing downhill,
arms
extended to their limit,
to
swim back up to the top
of
any bottomless water

Sad
that we so soon have
forgotten
as we constantly
reprimand:
No, No don't do that!
Verboten,
stay here in your yard

66 | Eventually

Eventually
the cooler air
stops,
ambient equals ambient

for a man
that
walked blind,
back

from cool,
the cave with
only
a solitary bat

asking
everyone met if
such
a difficult trip

could
be considered
worthy
in the final analysis

as
the bat's nose Eskimo-
Pies
in spite of us

67 | Paper

strange back light
impatient opposition
of flattened words

Thing of paper
on paper
for you

Silence of paper
moves away only
with fingers grip

not in unison
discord varies
without time

silence gains
until the encrypted
person lying on

page begins reading
out-loud, domestic
harmony clashes

or some one begins
to read those words
on a blank sheet

I should have
left you home
for quiets sake

68 | Truth Is

This feral growl,
loose sand's song,
twirls around sandals

why am I alone
listening to evocative
vanilla vocatives

truth is that
this brush, trees,
green grass even

are not supposed
to hold forever
open dune's gasps,

sliding cries, on
their way back to
where they came from

anyway and accumulate
their bookish weight
on an obliging crust

69 | Wait

Walt was the one
that showed
us how to list

but this will not
take as
long for you

If I could but
get into
your corpus callosum

with a trickle
of energy
I could show you

your past and future
where behind
all shadows you smell

death, and any movement
is your
inelegant father's

apparition seeking
a way out
careful to leave some

laughter, shrugging shoulders,
ink drops
and arrows pointing up

or down for an
uneasy audience
out of its own body